THE HOUSE
OF
EVERYTHING

THE HOUSE
OF
EVERYTHING

Robert Seatter

Seren is the book imprint of
Poetry Wales Press Ltd.
Suite 6, 4 Derwen Road, Bridgend,
Wales CF3 1HL

www.serenbooks.com
Facebook.com/SerenBooks
Twitter@SerenBooks

The right of Robert Seatter to be identified as the author
of this work has been asserted in accordance with the
copyright, Designs and Patents Act, 1988.

Collage artworks also by Robert Seatter
Design by Sally James

© Robert Seatter 2021

ISBN: 9781781725856

Ebook: 9781781725863

A CIP record for this title is available from
the British Library.

The publisher acknowledges the financial assistance of the
Books Council of Wales.

Cover art: 'Bocca della Verita' by Robert Seatter

Printed in Bembo by Pulsioprint, France

Introduction

This book is conceived as a navigation from
room to room of Sir John Soane's Museum,
taking in the Pompeian red Library, the Crypt
with its glowing alabaster sarcophagus of
Seti I, the Picture Room unfolding its
all-too-close-to-home story of a Rake's Progress,
the Monk's Parlour (dwelling of a completely
fictitious gothic monk), the airy delights of the
decorated Breakfast Room and right up to the
Turner-yellow Drawing Rooms.

The story of Soane is interwoven with the stories
of some of the extraordinary objects in the house,
collected from all around the world, as well as an
exploration of the impulse within us all to make
material our dreams and imaginings.

Acknowledgements

With many thanks to Sir John Soane's Museum
for being the inspiration behind this book,
and for giving me access to its secret places.

Thanks as ever to my generous friend Jane Duran
and the writers of the Wednesday Group for their
insightful criticism, and to Sally James for her
daring designer eye.

Contents

Not just the house we live in...

but the house we make up
in another language, in another country,
where we believe in different gods

and die quite differently.
Or simply a house in a foreign street
we like the look of, where the bakery smells

hang for longer — or so it seems —
in the morning air. Or maybe the house
where love is easy, that balance of intimacy

and space just so, and the peacock blue,
viridian green and egg-yolk yellow
are more vivid than before — like the world

glimpsed through coloured glass,
and our domestic objects with their own joint history
make a trail from room to room.

Or it's that house where we work
with depth and efficacy,
each hour so clear like a transparent cube

placed one on another, and our mind's eye there
is bright as a magnifying glass.
Or even the house we build, like this:

cantilevered in air, fixed solid in the London clay,
so we stand in this architrave and know
what we are made of and almost who we are.

*Soane bequeathed his unique house museum to the nation in 1833,
stipulating that it be kept 'as nearly as possible in the state in which he
shall leave it'. He consciously created a house of time and for all times.*

Pompeian Red

*Today, the PANTONE name is known worldwide as the standard language
for accurate colour communication: www.pantone.com.*

It's PANTONE 18-1658 TCX. *Easy to order now:
simply click, add to cart.* No need to travel

for weeks and months to a collapsed Italian city,
stooping to secrete a small fragment of red

in your travelling coat's deep pocket, touching it
now and then with your youthful finger.

*Pantone Pompeian red is available in a range
of Pantone products. Here are recommendations*

from our product suggestion team. But John,
you'd dreamt it already, hadn't you?

Those leather-bound books in a row,
those walls, that room – that deep, age-old red

surrounding you. *Durable colour
is formulated to maximize colour fastness.*

No need, no need, you held it in your hand,
your eye. Years passed, and that city rose,

resplendent red, out of your keen and purposeful
remembering.

---

*This is the largest room in the house, the walls of which are painted
Pompeian red. When Soane visited Pompeii as a young man on his
Grand Tour, he pocketed a fragment of wall plaster of this colour.*

Sir John Soane imagines the Ruins of His yet-to-be-built Building

Begin with the end:
the ruins, the picturesque pile
with only time's crenellations
left now in silhouette,
and every last window open
into air. Begin with the trees,
the roots, that slow creep
of moss – they were always there
at the corner of your eye,
and this clearing in the wood
only ever temporary. Begin
with the list of irksome lost things,
the accidents of memory
that must somehow be purposeful,
and love's strange collisions
that wake you in the night:
all the things that survive.

Bizarrely, Soane commissioned drawings of his own Bank of England buildings – utterly in ruins, in the gothic or ancient style.

Breakfast Parlour

Take morning light here –
hours of milk and marmalade.

Sip tea and honeysuckle,
cut triangles of white bread,

and live a constant summer –

for there's no snake in this garden,
no night to follow day:

here's a house to banish winter,
two lion dogs at the door

to bare their teeth
and howl away time.

*This small room is decorated with an ornate trompe l'œil ceiling, in
the form of a garden pergola, creating an illusion of perpetual leafiness.*

Lumière Mystérieuse

                    Gather it there –
on the wooden treads of the cantilevered

staircase going up/going down,
and in the turn of an ancient head –

there are so many, in multiple conversations –
over those rumpled curls where a finger

might fit so well. Or to and fro
among the one hundred mirror pieces,

fro and to, and then off again
into the elusive corridor of *somebody saw,*

somebody said: shuttlecock whispers.
Or go gather it outside, in the always winter

courtyard, peering through the smoke-yellow pane,
like one remembering a small and sudden

benign past, its moment warm on the nape
of a naked neck. Or stand here under the lantern glass –

caught like an unbusy bee in its amber light,
which is only time after all, mysteriously held.

Various areas of the house, but especially the Dome area, are lit by skylights of lemon yellow and darker amber glass, which create Soane's favourite atmospheric 'lumière mystérieuse' (mysterious light).

Empty Pistol Cabinet, 1696
or Playing *Cluedo* in
Sir John Soane's house

This is no ordinary country house to witness death.
Have you seen Peter the Great somewhere on the stairway,
pursuing Miss Scarlett, or in earnest conversation
with Professor Plum in the Shakespeare alcove...
how many children had the deceased Lady Macbeth?
Who stabbed who behind the arras in a so-called accident?
He has questions for every hour and there *is* an answer,
he is most insistent. While Mrs Peacock in the dark red library
stands practising her poses – has studied the flamboyancy
of the picture on the library wall, is a mistress of deception;
though in this house there's more than one discernible
snake in the grass. And Reverend Green? He's out the back,
exploring his faith with Father Giovanni, if there's light
to see it by. And the fragrant Mrs White, dressed in diaphanous
muslin, skin fine as porcelain, is upstairs in the morning room,
sipping English Breakfast tea, arranging the day's diary.
While you, the uninitiated visitor, wander the rooms,
in search of a message, a body, a plot. There were four
family members when the game began – till the figurines
cracked in their decorated box. Now Colonel Mustard lies down
on the first floor yellow carpet, his finger cocked
on the...Turkish captain's gun, yes the one that was missing
from the cabinet at this poem's beginning. Do you follow,
are you followed? Death is coming, that's the one thing certain
in a house like this: how to manoeuvre the body
down that narrow spiral staircase and into the sarcophagus
without anyone noticing? It's simply a matter of timing and time.

> *Crammed with objects, this room includes a mysteriously empty pistol*
> *case. The gun from it was stolen in the 1960s and never found –*
> *like a historic version of the game of* Cluedo.

The House of Everything

Everything must go in – fragments
of stained glass, ancient cornice and pedestal,
odd classical feet (human/animal), odd flowers
from the sea now solid as rock, great works
of the Italian masters in gilded frames –
their names like pasta sauces, their ten-a-penny idylls.
And sling in too the grimacing gargoyles
for easy contrast, hacked from facades
of windy cathedrals, a lank lock of hair
from a saint and a sinner (they are one
and the same), a missing pistol – its ricochet
bullet somewhere in these rooms. Everything,
everything. Now recite the list of what you
saved. Now the one thing you missed:
its gleaming plinth, its jealous empty space.

*Soane collected obsessively, the final collection in his house numbering
almost 50,000 objects, each meticulously catalogued before his death.*

I take my new lover to
Sir John Soane's Museum

to see if he likes it as much as I do (so a judgement
of sorts); to observe which space, which object,
he prefers (or would steal or own: we play that game too),
and to watch a half-blush, half-smile come over his face
as we turn to find Apollo's huge naked body
(cock concealed by the usual generous leaf)
suddenly looming over us: is it that one?;
to discover if we can make our bodies intimately fit –
by accidental design – up its winding staircase,
in its narrow corridors, or inside one of those sudden,
semi-obscure nooks *(This way/No, that way.*
Oh sorry/Sorry!); to catch his face in the amber-
gold light, so timeless it makes me wonder:
is this a face I can love now – a little longer than now?;
to ponder too on the curiosity of love
here in this cabinet of curiosities: so does love end
when the curiosity – of body, of mind – goes,
when we feel there is nothing new left to know?;
to lose him at the last moment in its trickery of spaces,
send him a text: *Has Mr Soane kidnapped you?*,
find him again with a sort of elated recognition:
You here? Yes, here – he blinks, I blink, my voice
outside myself calls from an upper room,
from beneath my feet, walks now quite deliberately
towards me – *Yes, here we are.*

The Rake's Progress

After Hogarth

So what's at the heart of the story?
Is it money? The debts piled up
on the green baize table, and that
illusory chink of gold to come – in the next

gilded picture – there at the fall
of the tumbling dice. Or new-fangled celebrity?
His freshly tailored peacock velvet suit
caught in the glare of their jealous eyes,

and his nacreous buttons winking right,
winking left, as he walks into every room.
Or is it sex, in the afternoon? Her petticoats
parted, a gape of flesh, and that flush of blood

up her neck to her lips. He wants that taste
of her again and again, while his body thrashes
like an electric eel. Or maybe it's love?
Surely that's there in the corner

of the very last picture? A father stands
quietly weeping for the son – or sons? –
he somehow lost, whose hearts now grey
and glassy flint were once so kind and tender.

The ingenious design of this room enabled Soane to display over one hundred pictures, including Hogarth's famous Rake's Progress sequence – the story of which bears an uncanny resemblance to the flawed life of Soane's own sons. He described them in his diary as 'These flinty-hearted sons'.

Padre Giovanni

I keep him there in the dark side
of the house, a place of winter walls
and birdless song. I spy him through

the amber glass, his regular to and fro
paces on stone, his muttered prayers
tipped into my ear, in a language I have tried

so hard to forget... Sometimes I invite him
to dine at my table – a place is laid for him
on cool, crisp linen, my best silver and china

taken out of store. But he never leaves
his shuttered room, the fish on his plate
watches me with its one glassy eye,
parts its dead lips, won't speak a word.

*Soane created this gothic space inhabited by a fictional monk called
'Padre Giovanni', who seems to reflect the dark and depressive side
of Soane's own nature.*

The Mansion of Woe
(after lonely walking)

Library of attitudes	*(one eye always watches)*
Dining Room of magnification	*(rooms inside rooms)*
Study of profundity	*(narrow, deep water)*
Dressing Room of assiduity	*(after elongation)*
Picture Room of morality/ immorality	*(yours for the choosing, sons of mine)*
Parlour of whimsicality	*(tea with the vicar and one small dog)*
Yard of isolation	*(prayers unanswered)*
Crypt of entertainment	*(after extensive illumination)*
Colonnade of curiosity	*(out of and into night)*
Dome of conviction	*(after long uncertainty)*
Breakfast Room of valour	*(my far-flung heroes)*
Staircase of breathlessness	*(polished pauses)*
Drawing Room of revelation	*(spread out on a table)*
Breakfast Parlour of illusions	*(one hundred bees and high summer)*

Shortly after the death of his wife in 1815, Soane wrote in his diary the poignant sentence: 'Dined as usual alone! Walked out in the evening for an hour and returned to my solitary cell! The Mansion of Woe.'

Winter Solstice in the House

We all know this place
in a winter solstice light,
at the darkest point of the year,

when there's no use in getting up
as the daylight hours are so short
and the rooms so loveless.

I could sleep here for years –
the air just my air,
no other's breath inside it –

and what to do with all I still have,
that's the hardest question
for this winter solstice hour,

what to do with all this unused love?

Breakfast with the Phrenologist

We surround him with noble heads –
Shakespeare, Kemble the actor, Emperor Augustus.

We watch his fingers with anticipation,
turning the conversation to nature, the noble savage,

the difficulty of hiring reliable servants in a house such as this.
We edge yet nearer with alternative heads –

Dr Dodd the forger, Cromwell's death mask,
the two sons of the Laocoon, their mouths a hollow

of silent agony. And we speak in empathetic symbols now –
this is the table of *truthfulness*, teapot of *benevolence*,

our windows are wide open to *mirthfulness* and *wonder*.
Anything to convince this German master.

Then we select and move closer more lustrous heads –
Pluto, Napoleon, myself John Soane –

observing his brow, its bright porcelain gleam,
sensing his twenty-seven organs jostling inside…

We are all *concentrativeness, cautiousness, ideality*,
and our left eyebrows twitch with recognizable *inhabitiveness*

as we slice the top off our speckled brown eggs,
let the egg yolk of our *amativeness* flow.

*This small, lower-ground space next to the crypt contains a table covered
with a variety of busts. Soane, like many of his contemporaries, was
captivated by the new 'head' science of phrenology, and once invited the
famous phrenologist Dr Spurzheimer to breakfast.*

Pasticcio

Believe in different gods
cantilevered in air, the list
of irksome lost things –
I have broken everything,
in search of a message, a body,
a plot, a door to let in
a river; but I don't remember
a word of the several languages
they say I spoke, fished
out of water, my arms and legs
given to a different story –
what is the forever truth?
I have broken everything,
here in the yard of isolation,
on the staircase of the breathless.
And do you ever dream
of what you lost?
Best not think of it at all,
I don't remember a word:
this calling in the dark,
the uncertainty of weather.
I have broken everything, re-
purposed here into some sort
of fixity: leafless, unmoving.

At the centre of this internal courtyard is 'the pasticcio', a column erected in
1819 and made up of separate architectural fragments. The poem imitates
this – with broken lines drawn from poems across the collection.

Sarcophagus

Like a boat left in a room
waiting for a door to let in a river,
for a current and for a paddle.

For a moon in a skylight,
waiting for a face to be dipped in milk,
for a marble and for a mirror.

For a dream left on a pillow,
waiting for a day to let in night,
for another door and for a key.

In 1824 Soane purchased the ancient Egyptian sarcophagus of Seti I.
Too expensive for the British Museum, Soane paid £2000 for it and
made it the centre piece of the sepulchral chamber in his 'museum house'.

Sir John Soane dreams of being mummified, in ten slow stages

1. Insert a hook through a hole near my nose,
   to pull out the brain,
   my over-busy, talkative brain.

2. Make a cut to the left side of my body,
   and remove all organs,
   all the tasting, turning, breathing parts of me.

3. Dry them with thoroughness, till they are just so much
   wrinkled bladderwrack left on the shore,
   and the sea long gone beyond the horizon.

4. Place my lungs, intestines, stomach, liver
   inside canopic jars and seal them tight,
   then set them aside – they are useless now.

5. Only put the hopeful heart back into the body,
   to purge it, crush it, so it can't feel a thing:
   what use feeling in this empty world?

6. Then rinse my body
   with spices, wine and thick layers of salt:
   corrosive, all-invasive salt.

7. After 40 days stuff with sand,
   give it the illusion of human shape –
   I say 'illusion' categorically, since I'm long left now.

8. Then 70 days later wrap it (not *I*)
   from head to toe in bandages – tighter, tighter –
   till I am no one, nowhere, nothing.

9. Place it in a wooden box, painted with gold leaf,
   criss-crossed black,
   and leave it in my waiting crypt.

10. One day, I hope not to wake from this dream.

Such Parties then in the Underworld

while the oil lamps burned
three long and crowded nights
and the house grew narrow;
tickets were on offer –
so I took the intimate boat trip
around the square, lost myself
in a pale green sycamore wood
where stars pricked the leaves
and a small dog wandered curious
under our feet; while I drank the purple-
coloured liquor from a foreign hill
(they showed me the spot
in one of those clever, fold-out paintings)
and I swallowed the tiny golden key
offered me on a spinning plate –
but I don't remember a word
of the several languages they say I spoke,
nor what happened to the rakish young man
in a beautiful white shirt (a left-over guest
from another party, and going to the bad
or so they said); though I remember you
in the press of the crowd and looking over
the curved balustrade – your scent
of bergamot, your mirror-brown eye –
those stories you told me
of the Doge of Venice who threw his ring
into the neat pleated waves, and for a moment
at that party I thought I caught
the glint of its here-and-gone gold.

To celebrate the arrival of the sarcophagus, Soane held three evening parties inviting nearly 1000 guests and illuminating the building with more than 300 oil lamps. Here's a youthful and imagined visitor's impressions.

Kiss Now

kiss now   let's do it   here
inspired by naked statuary   Apollo etc
he's so easy with his limbs   so unashamedly present
and can't you hear like me   the crocodile clock
of impending death?   tick   tock   tick   tock
kiss now   undo my shirt   unbuckle
my jeans before the kindly volunteer guide turns
to see us   don't worry he's deep in architectural
commentary so kiss now   make me come
death is for a long time   can't you hear tick tock?
let's not waste this January Tuesday   this space
we stepped into because of bad weather   the BBC's
unreliable forecast   kiss now   we share artistic
interests after all   a deep concern for the English
Enlightenment   tick   tock   kiss harder harder
death is forever   we are   almost naked
in the   corner half-light   half
way to death   tick   tock   kiss now

Soane's house, and more particularly the crypt, featured in a Henry James
novella, A London Life, where the heroine accidentally views her sister's
illicit assignation there while sheltering from a thunderstorm. The house
has an undeniably erotic charge.

The Museum After Hours

No longer passive, we speak now –
      in a slow bubble of conversation,

in all the languages: Greek, Latin, French,
      High German, Italian, Persian, Arabic…

and hundreds more, the noise of us rising
      like a cloud of bees.

Some of us want to chat:
      the time of day, the weather, odd bitchy comments
on that perpetual traffic of visitors…

Others want to debate: politics, religion,
      the universal nature of metaphor –

why death for you is sleep, a river,
      why for me it's an angel, a bird, a slow-burning pyre.

And some of us want a home
      to get back to, that place of belonging,

while others want only this constant tide of change:
      a traveller at the door, dusty and stateless,

saying *We are all the world's,*
      can we come in?

Bocca della Verita

Imagine Audrey here,
escaping on her moped with Gregory Peck –
beauty on the run, her princess accent,
her wind-ruffled hair, doing the things
that common people do in 1950s Roma:
eating *gelato*, dancing on the river bank.
The aching, sun-bleached, black-and-white glamour
of it all. Then everything stopping –
her small white hand slipped inside
the dark open mouth of the *Bocca della Verita* –

just like the one here. And the gods,
the saints, the dead celebrity
in his alabaster boat, the severed hands and feet,
the talking heads… all pause and listen
just like in the film: what is the forever truth?
But then Gregory pulls back her small white hand,
saves her from Soane – the dark gloating
of memory. Time enough for that.
There's Gregory's almost-kiss coming closer;
jazz of second improvised on second;
and the breath-stopping beauty
of her here-and-now profile against the light.

*On the walls of the Colonnade is 'a mouth of truth' from a Roman
fountain, similar to the one that famously features in Roman Holiday,
the 1953 film which made a star of the then unknown Audrey Hepburn.*

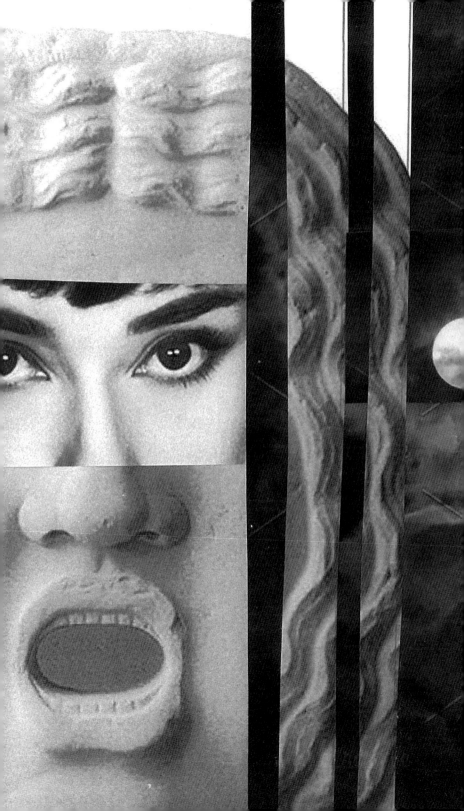

Sir John Soane reflects on his House as a Dream

Of course there is logic
and a cantilevered staircase,
but think of it – though I hate
to use the word – as a dream.
The man's face was fished
out of water, his arms and legs
given to another story,
so nothing need be complete.
Think of it as night in every room,
then the day will surprise you,
and when you ascend the staircase
imagine floating towards the light
as if you wore a diving suit
and your breath came back to you,
cased in glass, not quite your own.
Of course, there is religion,
and a holy man in a gothic grotto,
but belief is far from obligatory here,
and there are multiple roads
into this underworld,
and an attendant boat docked
at the quay. Think of it as a maze,
designed to confuse, structured
to delight, then the rooms
will become yours, the cupola
a crown you wear on your head,
balanced perfectly – and you,
you never even felt its soft
and momentary alighting.

Soane himself described his house as having 'a sequence of these fanciful effects that constitute the poetry of architecture'. It is indeed artful and highly wrought; it is also extraordinarily strange and surprisingly dream-like.

Ammonite

A winding staircase like a shell –
I put my ear to it and a building rises
like a dream. Space was never freer

than this: at the centre of the box tree
maze is a beating heart. Can you
hear it? Like a clock in a room –

the one where I am sitting, the one
where you draw the curtains
as outside the sea-green night descends.

Ammonites were prehistoric sea creatures, and there are a number of them at various places in the house. They in turn influenced the architecture of the house, in particular the spiraling cantilevered staircase.

Cantilevered

It's an act of will to believe in it.
    In fact, best not think about it at all –

a little like breathing or falling in love.
    So simply walk the projecting treads

in air, anchored at one end to the wall
    of the house, *terra firma*. Then imagine

every bridge, tower, football stadium
    built like this, as if they floated in air – and you

floating with them. And imagine too
    that skater – stage name Mr Frick –

long-time performer with the *Ice Follies Spectacle:*
    how he created 'the cantilever', his show-

stopping moment, would flex his knees,
    bend right backwards, then skate

in parallel to the ice. Oh the cold rush
    of air, the wonder of almost

but not quite touching!

The cantilevered staircase that winds up the tall, thin house is a structural and aesthetic triumph – seeming as it does to float in air.

For a staircase there must have been...

and a carpet   that I edged with my toe
followed upwards daily
with my eye

an armchair I sat in
to watch and understand the world
slowly becoming   its glazed and worn upholstery

a mirror that I smiled at and shaved in
practised wearing the face I wore
till it turned right into   the one I knew

a woman too who moved in the rooms above me
her familiar rhythms   the spaces in her breathing
her shadow bending on the blind

those children who hid behind the heavy curtains
then ran   towards me
opened my weary eyelids when I slept late on Sundays

a window that let in light
the uncertainty   of weather
the belief of bells

and a door that opened wide
to issue in   wonders
all manner of wonders

Soane wrote a very strange 'autobiography' of his house, called 'Crude Hints towards a History of My House', in which he imagines his house already in ruins and a 'very extensive assemblage of fragments'. The title of the poem is a fragmentary sentence, a brief annotation to the main text of this book.

Skeleton in the Closet

Can you hear me rattle
behind this plain wooden door?
In spite of iron rods jointing bone

to bone, tight binding of
wire, and a wedge of cork
between each countable vertebra?

I'm a coat-hanger man,
waiting for a jacket, a mackintosh,
a knot of paisley tie;

waiting to be even half-believable,
and longing for weather,
changeable weather.

Can you sense my wishing
with your x-ray vision?
This door after all is only wood,

merely physical matter
re-purposed into some sort of fixity:
leafless, unmoving.

I'm your closet cliché
transformed into fact –
that fleshless thing

you dance to avoid,
my fingers too bony,
my stare too hollow.

Soane kept a complete skeleton as a curiosity in the Monk's cell visible through a small window halfway down the back stairs. It had belonged to his friend, the sculptor John Flaxman, and is one of the more unusual memento moris that fill the house.

But this house's hide-and-seek game
will soon be over,
though you placed me here

then ran to safety –
crouched behind the statuary,
slipped into the bookcase –

oh I can sense
the breathing bundle
of your rush-about life –

and I'm the voice that is counting:
98, 99, 100. Coming…
Yes, you can be sure I am coming.

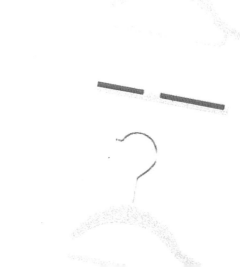

The Empty House

Such a little thing, this grief –
      where shall I hide it?

At the bottom of the garden
where the stream is stoppered,
the light turns green?

Or in the glazed rows of books
lined up inside the mirror's
nowhere space?

      No, not hidden enough.
How about the artifice
of that clever-clever picture gallery,

painting behind painting,
glory hiding glory?
No one will look there.

      No, I know where it must go –
in that tethered boat
waiting for departure

there in the basement –
its stretched out sleeper,
its indecipherable words…

Switch off the lights
as I climb inside
with my damp, untidy bundle –

      now open the door,
let the drowning river in.

Grieving for his wife, Soane made his house a sort of mausoleum to her memory and to his inconsolable sense of loss.

Mrs Soane's Tomb becomes a Telephone Box

I am a tomb
I am a phone box
I am dead
I am calling
from the other side
I am here:
insert your coins
(the way we once did),
dial my number
and when you hear
my opening words
press the button,
begin to speak –
I am waiting,
while your fingers fumble
on the other side,
I am waiting.

*In the library is a model of the tomb built for Mrs Soane in the burial
ground of St Giles-in-the-Fields (now St Pancras Gardens). The tomb
was the inspiration for the iconic red telephone box designed in the 1920s.*

Chère Amie

It's easier in another language, isn't it?
Easier to be so much more precise:

each word cut out separately
for scissor-sharp meaning,

and dangling foreign in familiar air –
I strove for that and said it. Easier too

to explain away this unfamiliar rush
of feeling, this calling in the dark:

I am not quite responsible after all –
those words don't quite belong to me,

that latinate lilt never of my shaping.
And perhaps easier at the last

to understand why no one answers:
silence/*silence* being sadly the same

in both our separate tongues...
But is there not in some other country

a language for me to learn, where I will
write to you and you will answer?

*Soane's beloved wife Eliza died in 1815. Under a pencil portrait of her he
wrote in French: Chère amie, je ne peux plus entendre ta voix–apprends
moi ce que je dois faire–pour remplir tes souhaits! ('Dear friend, I can no
longer hear your voice–teach me what I must do–to fulfil your wishes!')*

Salt and Rust

Shall we go backwards
through the story, begin
at the ending as he always
did: what's left, what's
remembered – the sediment
of what matters, there
on the beach, kicked up by the waves,
salvaged from so much
but surviving after all –
though a little corroded,
eaten by salt and rusted
at the edges, layered under sand –
the weight, oh the weight of it! –
yet appearing now,
heart-stoppingly fresh,
but was that really how it was?
shall we begin again
again to be entirely sure?

Soane was obsessed with what the past means, might mean. There were no
answers, no matter where or when he started.

The Collector's Anxiety Dream

I have broken everything –
'magnificent fragment' says
the museum caption on every object.
And I have only six and a half hours –
my sleeping time, for I have nights now
of briefer and briefer sleeping –
to gather all the fragments,
glue them together, place them back
in their decorative niches
and spotlit hollows
and re-write the caption
of each small white label.
I walk the stairways, walk the halls –
there's the crunch of fragments
underfoot, fragments on fragments –
then someone arrives with a ticking clock
and a box of colour-coded treasury tags.
So what, I ask, *do I do*
with the treasury tags?

A sense of the broken and the irreparable dominates Soane's manuscript
called 'Crude Hints towards a History of My House', in which he imagines
his house a 'very extensive assemblage of fragments'. The persistent question
of this book is how to capture what is ruined and lost.

On the Road to Europe

Yes – there are many things in my house,
and some days I believe in them.

I, with my meticulous fingers,
my room filled with cork models

of antiquity, my memories commissioned
in water colour, I, yes, I.

And then some days I wake
from a dream of emptiness

here in this house
where there is not one thing…

I have lost my trunk
on the glittering roads of Europe:

Florence, Venice, Rome –
the cities rise before me,

I am 20 years old again,
and I must hold these things

here in the fire of my shaping imagination
where everything is made.

As a young man on his Grand Tour, Soane lost his trunk containing the books and artefacts he had collected on his journey. It would prefigure losses to come later in his life.

The Man who destroyed everything he had meets Sir John Soane

He made an inventory of 300 pages
in ten categories:
artworks,
clothing,
electrical equipment,
furniture,
kitchenware,
leisure items,
motor vehicles,
perishables,
reading materials,
studio materials.

7,227 items in all
including even the following:
his passport and birth certificate,
clothing (his father's sheepskin coat among them),
works of art (Tracey Emin, Damien Hirst etc)
and his Saab 900 Turbo 16S.
The resulting bags of granulated rubbish
weighed nearly six tonnes
and were all recycled or sent to landfill.
Nothing remained,

In 2001, artist Michael Landy painstakingly catalogued all his possessions
then destroyed them: "I'm always trying to get rid of myself" he said.
Here, I imagine his encounter with Soane, the obsessive collector.

or rather all that remained was nothing.
Do you ever dream of what you lost?
asked John Soane,
as he walked the winding staircase
of his crammed house
touching his treasured possessions
one by one.

Do you ever dream of an empty house?
asked the other,
walking out of it,
yourself on an empty road,
carrying nothing
but the clothes on your back
listening to the sound of your breathing –
how the horizon lifts
and trembles…?

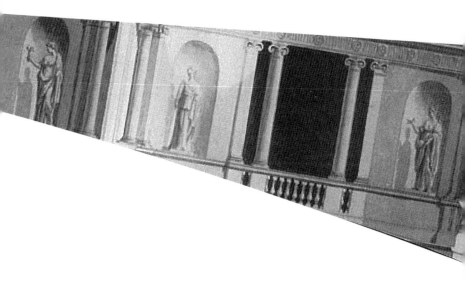

Papercut of Sir John Soane's Museum

This is the house
inside out.

These are the lives
carefully scissored.

And those the silhouettes
in intimate detail –

so here is intelligence,
culture, beauty

in the line of a brow,
wave of hair,

fuss of lace
and stiff brocade.

But mostly this is the blade
lonely, loving

and close to blood.

Teasels

Their heads are everywhere in this house,
on almost every chair
in almost every room –
and indeed, Wikipedia tells me
they are considered an invasive species,
form a monoculture, capable of crowding out
the other plants.

But here they are placed with a silent message:
don't sit on this seat, don't caress with your hand
this mahogany table.
They prickle with the delicate reminder
of place and time,
will not last the passage of too many
human bodies and hands.

Yet put them out in the garden air
at the back of this house,
and they'd gather rain water in the leaves
at their stem.
They'd stand tall with their seed head,
a tight packed larder.
They'd feed the small bright winter birds.

This house is now a museum, and the traffic of our feet and hands takes its constant toll on the fabric of the place. Teasel heads are placed everywhere to remind us not to touch or sit.

Memento

Leave via the gift shop,
buy a memory
of memory – perhaps a ceramic house,
forty centimetres high:
your very own Soane.

Purchase a mirror
of a mirror to slip in your bag:
you'll never escape
the way light bends here,
these peacock eyes.

Slip a mystery
of mystery between your shirt cuffs –
small procession of hieroglyphs,
or read the Book of the Dead
all down your silk tie.

And take a stranger
for strangeness – there's a colour-coded map
for the lost and the wandering,
walk in and out of shadows:
meet yourself there.

What do you take away from this strange and unique house?
There are tangible and intangible things...

Sparrow in Sir John Soane's Museum

I imagine it curious, tap-tapping
its small, non-descript beak against the glass,
then I imagine it devious slipped through
a crevice, in through a loose 18th century tile.
I imagine it flying through these extraordinary
rooms, an ordinary sparrow dazed
by eyeless statuary, in love with cool marble
and seduced by the curvature of mirror walls.
I imagine it singing in the make-believe spring
of a *trompe l'œil* landscape, sun on its wings,
plentiful grapes for the picking, and its egg
the mottled grey of a painterly sky.
And I imagine it dying in captioned glory,
its name in Latin like a small parcelled prayer.

*Something of Soane's humble beginnings – he was the son of a builder –
is captured here in the imagined apparition of a sparrow, lost then trapped
within the alluring house's walls.*

Coda: **Present Perfect Continuous**

I have been coming here for years –
that is the most complicated of English tenses,
which my poor Italian students stuttered over
when I taught them English in Milan.
It's the past connecting to the present
then running into the future. It's a river
under this city, now paved over and lost,
but rushing on, the dark messy pulse of it.
It's love underneath so many daily words
and actions, making them matter
so they glow a little around the edges,
and hurt sometimes too – since finding
and losing and finding again can do that.
It's this house caught in the weight of this
or that object, the light falling on them
then slowly wheeling on, and the young man I was
when I first stepped into its narrow hallway –
I'd seen the poster on the tube, its collage
of heads and patterns that intrigued,
and knocked one late school day afternoon
on its I'm-not-giving-away-anything door –
to the biographer I have become,
connecting the cut-out moments of a life,
repeating the walk from room to room,
climbing that giddy cantilevered stair
year on year. So this is who I was and am,
this house seems to say, and perhaps will be.

A short history of
Sir John Soane's Museum

Sir John Soane's Museum is the extraordinary house and museum of the British architect Sir John Soane (1753-1837).

Though born into relative poverty, as the fourth son of a bricklayer, Soane went on to become one of the foremost architects of the Regency era. He was particularly celebrated for his inventive use of light, space and his experimentation with forms of Classical architecture. As a result, he won numerous high-profile commissions of the day, including the Bank of England and Dulwich Picture Gallery, and created his own extraordinary home and museum on Lincoln's Inn Fields.

Today, Sir John Soane's Museum occupies three buildings, Nos 12, 13, and 14 Lincoln's Inn Fields. During his lifetime, Soane acquired and rebuilt each of these buildings. One of the driving impulses behind this expansion was the housing of his evolving collection of 'curiosities'. This featured everything from Roman sculpture and Egyptian antiquities – including the star object of the sarcophagus of Seti I – to models of contemporary buildings.

Soane never stopped arranging and rearranging this collection, as new objects appeared and as he delighted in creating ever-shifting and poetic juxtapositions. On his death in 1837, Soane bequeathed his house to the nation, on the understanding that it would be preserved exactly as it was at the time of his death, in perpetuity.

For further information go to **www.soane.org**